THE OXFORD BOOK OF

Funeral and Memorial Music for Organ

Compiled by
Julian Elloway

MUSIC DEPARTMENT

OXFORD
UNIVERSITY PRESS

OXFORD

UNIVERSITY PRESS

Great Clarendon Street, Oxford OX2 6DP,
United Kingdom

Oxford University Press is a department of the University of Oxford.
It furthers the University's objective of excellence in research, scholarship,
and education by publishing worldwide. Oxford is a registered trade mark of
Oxford University Press in the UK and in certain other countries

© Oxford University Press 2018

First published 2018

Impression: 1

ISBN 978–0–19–340119–8

Music and text origination by Katie Johnston
Printed in Great Britain on acid-free paper by
Halstan & Co. Ltd, Amersham, Bucks.

CONTENTS

Manual indications within the pieces of this collection are shown as Roman numerals as follows: I (= Gt.), II (= Sw.), and III (= Ch.).

There is much overlap between music used at funerals and weddings—in hymns and organ music. Many quieter pieces suitable for playing before a wedding or during the signing of the registers are also suitable at funerals. *The Oxford Book of Wedding Music* includes a further four arrangements of J. S. Bach; Boëllmann's *Prière à Notre-Dame*; two Airs and a Minuet by Handel; and Vaughan Williams's *Greensleeves* among many other pieces. It is a companion volume to this one.

A Grand Dirge

THOMAS ATTWOOD
(1765–1838)
ed. Julian Elloway

Largo assai

Written for Nelson's funeral in St Paul's Cathedral on 9 January 1806.

Chorale Prelude on
'Herr Gott, nun schleuss den Himmel auf'

('Lord God, now open up the heavens')

J. S. BACH (1685–1750)
BWV 617

Chorale Prelude on 'Liebster Jesu, wir sind hier'

(Canon at the 5th)

('Dearest Jesus, we are here')

J. S. BACH (1685–1750)

BWV 633

Chorale Prelude on
'Mit Fried und Freud ich fahr dahin'

('With peace and joy I depart')

J. S. BACH (1685–1750)
BWV 616

Chorale Prelude on 'Nun danket alle Gott'

('Now thank we all our God')

J. S. BACH (1685–1750)
BWV 657

Sonatina

from *Gottes Zeit ist die allerbeste Zeit* ('Actus Tragicus')

('God's time is the very best time')

J. S. BACH (1685–1750)
arr. Julian Elloway
BWV 106

* On a three-manual instrument it can be effective to alternate phrases between two different flutes.

Sinfonia

from *Ich steh' mit einem Fuss im Grabe*

('I stand with one foot in the grave')

J. S. BACH (1685–1750)
arr. Julian Elloway
BWV 156

Alternatively the LH may be played an octave lower on a suitable 4-foot stop.

* Bach's adaptation of the oboe melody in a harpsichord concerto, ten years later, shows much elaboration specific to that instrument. Organists, however, may like to consider some of the ornamentation and melodic variants.

Ave Maria

I: Solo
II: Light 8', 4'
Ped.: Soft 16', 8'

J. S. BACH (1685–1750)
and CHARLES GOUNOD (1818–93)
arr. Christopher Morris

Chorale Prelude on
'O wie selig seid ihr doch, ihr Frommen'

('O how blessed are you, the righteous')

JOHANNES BRAHMS
(1833–97)
Op. 122 No. 6

Molto moderato

How lovely are thy dwellings

('Wie lieblich sind deine Wohnungen')

from *Ein deutsches Requiem*, Op. 45

JOHANNES BRAHMS (1833–97)
arr. Julian Elloway

Mässig bewegt (with moderate movement)

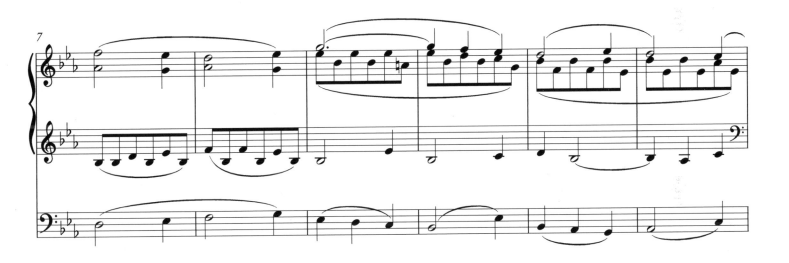

Nimrod

from *Variations on an Original Theme* ('Enigma Variations'), Op. 36

EDWARD ELGAR (1857–1934)
arr. Robert Gower

for Philippa

Desiderium

A Spiritual Quodlibet: *Steal away*; *Deep river*; *Swing low, sweet chariot*

ROBERT GOWER
(b. 1952)

Unhurried, with deep feeling and very freely ♩ = 60

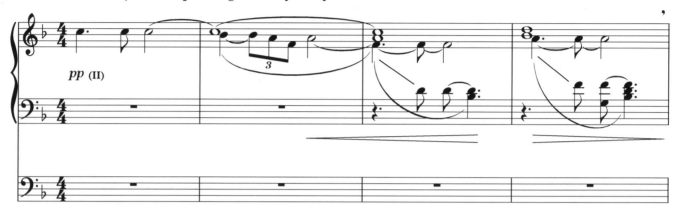

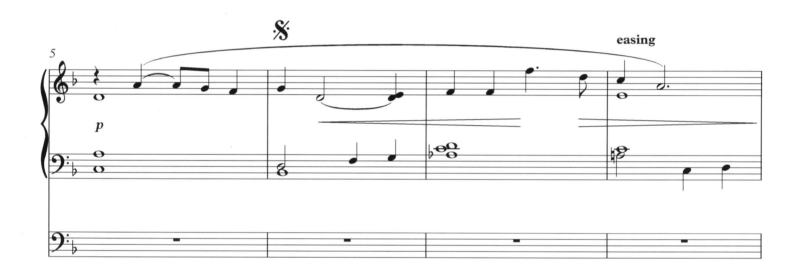

Pavane

Op. 50

GABRIEL FAURÉ (1845–1924)
arr. Julian Elloway

Andante molto moderato ♩ = 84

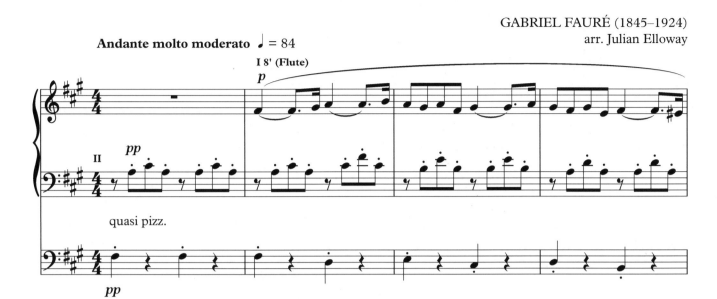

Largo

from Symphony No. 9 in E minor ('From the New World'), Op. 95

ANTONÍN DVOŘÁK (1841–1904)
arr. Julian Elloway

I know that my Redeemer liveth

from *Messiah*, HWV 56

G. F. HANDEL (1685–1759)
arr. Robert Gower

This piece may be played throughout as a trio, using contrasting stops in the right hand for the ritornellos and solos. Alternatively, both hands may play on the same manual for the ritornellos, the right hand then taking a separate manual for the solos as marked. Small notes provide optional harmony for cadences. A shorter version can be played by ending on the first beat of bar 75.

* End here for the shorter version.

Ombra mai fu

from *Serse*

G. F. HANDEL (1685–1759)
arr. Julian Elloway
HWV 40

O rest in the Lord

('Sei stille dem Herrn')

from *Elijah*, Op. 70

FELIX MENDELSSOHN (1809–47)
arr. Julian Elloway

For the Little Organ Book

C. HUBERT H. PARRY
(1848–1918)

Chorale Prelude on 'Eventide'

('Abide with me; fast falls the eventide')

C. HUBERT H. PARRY
(1848–1918)

Pavane pour une infante défunte*

MAURICE RAVEL (1875–1937)
arr. Julian Elloway

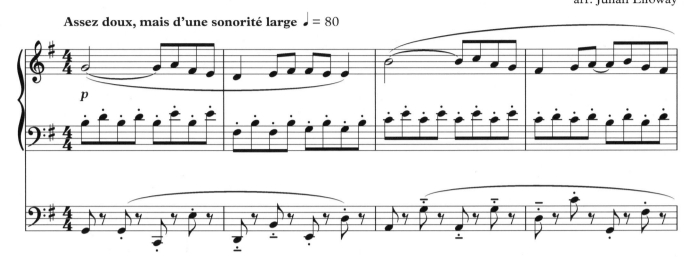

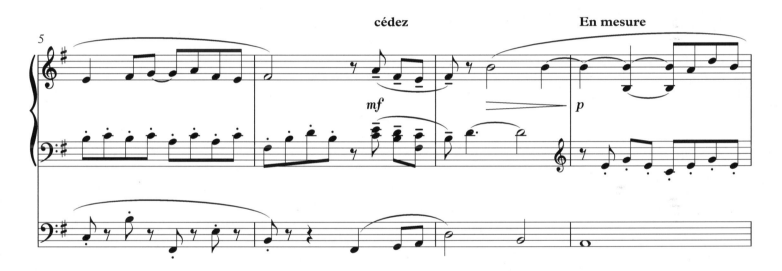

* i.e. for a dead princess ('infanta').

The tempo marking shown is from Ravel's original piano score. The later orchestral version was published with **Lent** ♩ = 54.

Gymnopédie No. 1

ERIK SATIE (1866–1925)
arr. Julian Elloway

Lent et douloureux

Organ arrangement in memoriam Suzanne Leighton

Adagio

from String Quintet in C major, D. 956

FRANZ SCHUBERT (1797–1828)
arr. Julian Elloway

Andante con moto

from String Quartet No. 14 in D minor ('Death and the Maiden'), D. 810

FRANZ SCHUBERT (1797–1828)
arr. Christopher Morris

Bist du bei mir

from *Notebook for Anna Magdalena Bach* (1725)

('If you are with me, I go with gladness')

G. H. STÖLZEL (1690–1749)
arr. Julian Elloway

for Victoria Ries

Contemplation on 'On Eagle's Wings'

MICHAEL JONCAS (b. 1951)
arr. Rebecca Groom te Velde

Prelude on 'Crimond'

('The Lord's my Shepherd, I'll not want')

REBECCA GROOM TE VELDE
(b. 1956)

Berceuse (sur les paroles classiques)

No. 19 from *24 Pièces en style libre*, Op. 31

II: 8' Gamba + Voix celeste;
I: 8' Flute; Ped.: 16' + 8';
II to I, II to Ped.

LOUIS VIERNE
(1870–1937)

Folk Tune

No. 2 from *Five Short Pieces*

PERCY WHITLOCK
(1903–46)